Who Pooped in the Sonoran Desert?

Written by Gary D. Robson

Illustrated by Robert Rath

FARCOUNTRY
PRESS

To Heather and Tré: Keep on asking questions!
- Gary

For Lucy and Thomas, my poop experts.
- Robert

ISBN 13: 978-1-56037-349-0
ISBN 10: 1-56037-349-0

© 2006 by Farcountry Press
Text © 2006 by Gary D. Robson
Illustrations © 2006 by Farcountry Press

For more information on our books,
write Farcountry Press, P.O. Box 5630, Helena, MT 59604;
call (800) 821-3874; or visit www.farcountrypress.com.

Book design by Robert Rath.
Created, produced, and designed in the United States.

Manufactured by
Everbest Printing (Guangzhou) Co. Ltd.
334 Huanshi Road South
Dachong Western Industrial District
Panyu, Guangdong, China
in June 2013
Printed in China.

17 16 15 14 13   5 6 7 8 9

Library of Congress Cataloging-in-Publication Data

Robson, Gary D.
    Who pooped in the Sonoran Desert? : scat and tracks for kids / written by Gary Robson ; illustrated by Robert Rath.
        p. cm.
    ISBN-13: 978-1-56037-349-0
    ISBN-10: 1-56037-349-0
    1. Animal tracks—Sonoran Desert—Juvenile literature. I. Rath, Robert, ill. II. Title.
    QL768.R647 2005
    591.75409791'7—dc22
                    2005030111

"Are we there yet?" Michael squirmed in the back seat. "We've been driving through the desert forever!"

3

"The Sonoran Desert is huge, Michael," replied Dad.

"There are lots of places to stop and hike," added Mom, "like Saguaro National Park, Organ Pipe Cactus National Monument, and a lot of other parks. There's a hiking trail up ahead."

the STRAIGHT POOP

The Sonoran Desert covers parts of Arizona and California in the United States, and parts of Sonora and Baja California in Mexico.

PACIFIC OCEAN

SAN DIEGO

FLAGSTAFF

CALIFORNIA

ARIZONA

PHOENIX

Tonto
National
Monument

Casa Grande Ruins
National Monument

SONORAN
DESERT

Sonoran Desert
National Monument

Ironwood Forest
National Monument

Saguaro
National
Park

TUCSON

Organ Pipe Cactus
National Monument

Arizona-Sonora
Desert Museum

BAJA
CALIFORNIA

GULF
OF
CALIFORNIA

NOGALES

SONORA,
MEXICO

5

"Michael's too scared to hike," said Emily. "He thinks a mountain lion's gonna eat him." She curved her fingers like claws and growled at Michael.

"Stop it, Emily," said Mom. "Nobody's getting eaten by anything."

6

Michael was excited about the trip,
but Emily was right.

He had just read a book about desert
wildlife, and the mountain lions
were scary!

"I *am* kind of scared of mountain lions," admitted Michael.

"Don't worry," Dad told him. "Mountain lions tend to stay away from people."

"Besides, we're going to show you how to learn all about them without ever getting close!" Mom added.

the STRAIGHT
POOP

Never hike by yourself. Mountain lions almost never bother people hiking in groups.

"Here's our first trail, kids," said Dad. "Let's see if we can spot some sign and we'll show you what we mean."

"Sign?" said Michael. "You mean like a sign at the zoo?"

"By the word 'sign,' we mean a clue that an animal has left behind, Michael," said Mom.

"Like this pile of poop?" giggled Emily.

"Well, yes, but trackers and hikers call it 'scat' instead of poop," said Dad with a smile.

"Who pooped here?" Michael asked. "It looks like the bunny poop we find in Velvet's cage at home."

"This looks like jackrabbit scat," Dad replied.

"And I think these are jackrabbit tracks over here," Mom added.

the STRAIGHT POOP

Jackrabbits aren't really rabbits; they're hares. Hares are bigger than rabbits and have longer ears and back legs than rabbits.

"See, Michael," said Dad. "We don't have to get up close to an animal to learn about it. Instead of a close encounter of the scary kind, we'll have a close encounter of the poopy kind."

Everybody laughed, and Mom made a gross-out face.

"Let's see if we can find some more animals," said Emily. She was having fun looking for clues.

"I found more scat," said Michael, trying to sound grown-up. "It's from a really big rabbit!"

"This isn't rabbit scat," Dad said. "It's from a deer."

13

DEER SCAT

JACKRABBIT SCAT

JELLYBEANS

"How can you tell?" Emily asked.

"Rabbit and hare scat is small and round, like little balls," Mom explained. "Deer scat is shaped more like jellybeans."

the STRAIGHT POOP

Rabbits eat their own scat! They do this to get as much nutrition from the food as they can. The little brown balls are scat that's already been through twice.

"Here are some deer tracks, too," said Dad.

"And an antler," said Michael. "Oh, no! Does that mean a mountain lion ate the deer?"

"The deer is fine," Dad said. "Deer shed their antlers every year, and then grow new, bigger ones."

the STRAIGHT POOP
Only male deer, called bucks, grow antlers.

15

"The antler is from a mule deer," said Mom. "You can tell by the shape."

the STRAIGHT POOP

Mule deer antlers split into even branches, while white-tailed deer antlers have points rising off of a big main "beam."

MULE DEER

WHITE-TAILED DEER

"Who pooped here?" yelled Michael. "This stuff is even bigger! Is it from a big mountain lion?" He tried not to sound scared.

"That scat is from a wild burro," said Mom.

Michael relaxed and looked at the ground again.
"There are footprints here, too," he said.

"Right," said Mom. "Just like a horse's hoofprints, only smaller."

the STRAIGHT POOP

It's easy to tell a burro from a horse: a burro is smaller and has a white muzzle, black edges around its ears, and black fur in the shape of a cross on its shoulders.

the STRAIGHT POOP

Horses and burros can poop and walk at the same time, but they have to stop and stand still to pee.

"Horses and burros were brought to America hundreds of years ago by early settlers. Many got away and formed wild herds," Mom told the kids.

"This cactus is gigantic," said Emily.

"That's a saguaro cactus," Dad replied. "They can live to be more than 200 years old, and grow as tall as a 5-story building!"

"Lots of animals live in saguaros," added Mom, "like those Gila woodpeckers."

the STRAIGHT POOP

Saguaro is a Spanish word. It's pronounced sa-WA-roe. The saguaro's blossom is the official Arizona state flower.

the STRAIGHT POOP

Gila is a Spanish word. It's pronounced HEE-la.

20

"Who pooped here?" asked Emily. "There are tracks next to the scat, but they're just smudges in the dirt."

Dad studied the scat. "I'm not sure, Emily, but it might be from a desert tortoise."

"It's definitely a desert tortoise," said Mom. "And there it is."

The family rushed over to look.

"Where's its pond?" asked Emily.

"Tortoises don't live in ponds like turtles," Mom answered. "They live in burrows in the ground."

"Look at that huge lizard!" said Michael.

"That's a chuckwalla," said Dad. "They can get up to a foot and a half long, but they're usually very shy."

23

"These look kind of like deer tracks," said Emily, "but they're smaller and not as pointy."

"The scat is different, too," added Michael. "What kind of animal left this?"

24

"Those are collared peccary tracks," said Mom.

"That's a funny name," Emily giggled.
"What's a peccary?"

"They're kind of like wild pigs. If you see any, don't get close. They can be bad-tempered," answered Dad.

the STRAIGHT POOP

Many people living in the Sonoran Desert call the collared peccary a "*javelina*" (pronounced *have-a-LEE-na*), which is the name for it in Mexico.

"Speaking of not getting close," said Mom, "there's a Gila monster over there."

"A monster!?" said Michael and Emily together. Michael looked scared.

"They aren't really monsters, that's just their name," Dad told the kids.

"Gila monsters are the biggest lizards in America," said Mom, "and they're venomous. They're generally calm and slow moving. Just stay away from them and you'll be fine."

the STRAIGHT POOP

Gila monsters and Mexican beaded lizards are the only venomous lizards in the world. They eat small animals, birds, and eggs.

The word "venomous" means that they produce a kind of poison.

"What's in that crack in the rocks?" asked Michael.

"That's a bat cave," replied Mom.

"I know what bat poop is called," said Emily. "We learned about it in school. Bat poop is called guano!"

the STRAIGHT POOP

Unlike the white, runny kinds of guano produced by some bats, these bats have poop that looks like mouse scat. This is because they eat insects instead of nectar.

"Right!" said Dad. "And when the sun goes down, you can see bats flying around and eating bugs."

the STRAIGHT POOP

These bats are called cave myotis. They use sonar to find meals at night. They make high-pitched squeaks and listen for the sound to echo off of a tasty treat like a flying moth.

"Who pooped on this tree? Is this more bat guano?" asked Emily.

"These white streaks are owl scat," said Mom. "See these tracks with two toes pointing forward and two pointing back, and the owl pellets around the base of the tree?"

"Owl pellets?" said Emily.

"Owls eat their prey whole," explained Mom. "The parts they can't digest, like hair and bones, get coughed up in a pellet like this."

the STRAIGHT POOP

Studying owl pellets is a great way to find out what owls eat. They dine on small animals such as mice, birds, and lizards. Sometimes you can see a small skull or other bones in the pellets.

"Yuck!" said the kids.

the STRAIGHT POOP

O wls see very well at night, but they aren't blind during the day, as some people think. They see just fine then, too.

"If you listen at night," said Dad. "You can hear barn owls making a hissing noise, instead of hooting like other owls."

Nearby, Michael spotted a pile of scat. "I found some big poop, I mean *scat*,"
he said, "and some tracks."

He looked around nervously. "This isn't from a mountain lion, is it?"

Dad walked over and looked. "Don't worry, Michael," he said. "This is coyote sign."

the STRAIGHT POOP

You can tell what a coyote has been eating by looking at its scat. Coyote scat often has hair and bits of bones in it that their bodies can't digest—that's how you can tell coyote poop from dog poop.

"These look like dog tracks," said Emily.

"That's because coyotes are in the dog family," explained Dad.

the STRAIGHT POOP

They're often called ringtail cats or civet cats, but ringtails aren't cats at all. They're related to raccoons.

Michael spotted a track that was different than the others he had seen.

"It looks like the coyote track, but it has more toes, and there's an extra mark in back," Michael said.

"That extra pad gives it away," said Dad. "It tells you that you are looking at a ringtail track."

Emily's eyes lit up. "Ringtails are cool! I love those big eyes. Do you think we'll see one?"

"I doubt it," replied Mom. "Ringtails are nocturnal, which means they sleep during the day and come out at night."

"Spider!" the kids yelled.

"You two found a tarantula," said Dad. "Don't worry—it won't bother you if you don't bother it."

"They're very pretty spiders," added Mom. "But they do bite."

the STRAIGHT POOP

There's a type of wasp called a tarantula wasp that kills tarantula spiders.

"Are these more ringtail tracks?" Emily asked. "They look different."

"Let's figure it out," Dad answered. "These tracks are a lot bigger, they don't have the extra pad in the back, and the claws are longer.

"They're coati tracks," said Mom, "and I think I hear some coatis just over that ridge."

"They sure do make a lot of noise," said Emily as they peeked at the troop.

38

They snuck away quietly, without disturbing the coatis.

the STRAIGHT POOP

Coatis (pronounced *co-WAH-tees*) are relatives of raccoons and ringtails. They hang out in troops, and you can hear them chatter, whine, grunt, and even scream as they talk to each other.

the STRAIGHT POOP

Coatis eat different types of food, including insects, lizards, and fruit. Their scat looks very different depending on what they've been eating.

39

"I think I found another coyote track," said Michael.

"That's not a coyote track," said Mom.
"It doesn't show any claw marks, and
you can see the 'leading toe' in the tracks.
It looks like you found your mountain lion."

"Oh, no! Where?" Michael gasped.

"I mean you found mountain lion *sign*,"
said Mom.

the STRAIGHT POOP

Since cats can retract their claws, their tracks don't show claw marks. Dog tracks often show claw marks.

COYOTE TRACKS

LEADING TOE

MOUNTAIN LION TRACKS

40

"Let's see what you two learned today," said Dad. "What can you figure out about this cat?"

"I see a bunch of scratch marks on this tree," said Emily. "I think it used it like a scratching post to sharpen its claws!"

the STRAIGHT POOP

Mountain lions have different names in different parts of the country. They're also called panthers, painters, cougars, pumas, and catamounts.

"Is this mountain lion scat?" asked Michael.

"It sure is," said Dad. "See how it tried to bury the scat?"

"It has lots of hair and bone in it, just like the coyote scat," Michael pointed out. "They definitely eat other animals."

the STRAIGHT
POOP

Mountain lions may be the biggest cat in America, but they still sometimes bury their scat just like a house cat.

Emily laid her hand next to the track.
"It must be very big," she said.

"That's right," Mom said. "A mountain lion
weighs as much as I do, and a big one can
weigh more than Dad!"

As they got back in the car, everyone talked about how much fun they had on the hike.

"We didn't see very many animals," said Emily, "but it seemed like we did!"

Everyone laughed when Michael said, "And I didn't get scared once!"

TRACKS and

MOUNTAIN LION

Four-toed tracks are bigger than a coyote's, but claws don't show. Big, center pad is dented. "Leading toe" shows in tracks.

Scat is rarely seen because they bury it.

COYOTE

Tracks are like a dog's, with four toes, usually with visible claw marks.

Scat is very dark colored with tapered ends and usually contains hair.

BLACKTAIL JACKRABBIT

Small tracks are filled in between the toes.

The scat is in little balls.

COATI

Tracks show five bulbous toes with long claws.

Scat is usually long cylinders.

RINGTAIL

Five toes on each foot, with claws often not showing.

Scat crumbles easily and often has insect parts in it.

SCAT NOTES

MULE DEER

Pointy tracks with split hooves.

Scat is oval-shaped like jellybeans, not round like a rabbit's.

COLLARED PECCARY OR JAVELINA

Shorter stride than a deer. Tracks are usually six to ten inches apart, not as pointed as deer tracks.

Scat is typically in large, uneven chunks.

BURRO

Tracks are much bigger than deer or peccary tracks, and not split.

Scat is in chunks, with roughage from vegetation often visible.

BARN OWL

Tracks show four toes: two pointing forward and two backward or sideways.

Scat is runny and white. "Cough pellets" contain fur and bones.

DESERT TORTOISE

Tracks are basically just round dents with sand or dirt heaped up behind.

Scat is 1 to 2 inches long, smooth, and tapered at both ends.

ABOUT the AUTHOR and ILLUSTRATOR

GARY ROBSON lives in Montana near Yellowstone National Park, where he and his wife own a bookstore and tea bar. Gary has written dozens of books and hundreds of articles, mostly related to science, nature, and technology.
www.robson.org/gary

ROBERT RATH is a book designer and illustrator living in Bozeman, Montana. Although he has worked with Scholastic Books, Lucasfilm, and Montana State University, his favorite project is keeping up with his family.

BOOKS IN THE
WHO POOPED IN THE PARK?™
SERIES:

Acadia National Park
Big Bend National Park
Black Hills
Cascades
Colorado Plateau
Death Valley National Park
Glacier National Park
Grand Canyon National Park
Grand Teton National Park
Great Smoky Mountains National Park
Northwoods
Olympic National Park
Red Rock Canyon National Conservation Area
Rocky Mountain National Park
Sequoia and Kings Canyon National Parks
Shenandoah National Park
Sonoran Desert
Yellowstone National Park
Yosemite National Park